The Beyerhaus Effect

An Outline of Contemporary Subversion

Frits Albers

July 1976

Edited by Frank Calneggia

En Route Books and Media, LLC
Saint Louis, MO

⊛ENROUTE
Make the time

En Route Books and Media, LLC
5705 Rhodes Avenue
St. Louis, MO 63109

Contact us at
contactus@enroutebooksandmedia.com

Cover Credit: Sebastian Mahfood

Copyright 2026 Michael P. Albers

ISBN-13: 979-8-88870-503-2
Library of Congress Control Number: 2026933920

All rights reserved. No part of this book may be reproduced, stored in a retrieval system, or trans- mitted in any form, or by any means, electronic, mechanical, photocopying, or otherwise, without the prior written permission of the author.

Table of Contents

Editors Preface: A Tribute to Professor Dr. Peter Beyerhaus 1

Introduction 5

Chapter One: The Ingredients of 'Spiritual Marxism' 11

Chapter Two: The Detection and Destruction of 'Spiritual Marxism' 57

Conclusion 77

Editor's Preface

A Tribute to Professor Dr. Peter Beyerhaus

(1 February 1929 to 18 January 2020)

The 'Front Line Mission South Africa' presents its tribute to Prof Beyerhaus with these words:

"South Africa will probably never fully appreciate how much she owes to Professor Peter Beyerhaus, for he accompanied her through dangerous times. Our country has experienced a revolution, which has changed her from a Christian to a secular country and this turn-about was effected mainly by the World Council of Churches.

"In 1974, Prof Beyerhaus came to South Africa by invitation of The Christian League to give a series of lectures on Missiological and Ecumenical Developments within the

Church. Based on his book, *"Kingdom of God or World Community?"* (*Reich Gottes oder Weltgemeinschaft?*), he spoke about the *"Berlin Declaration"* (*Berliner Ökumene-Erklärung*) and warned against the utopian vision of the World Council of Churches. He pointed out the unBiblical aspects of the World Council of Churches and its South African satellites. Their programmes had become ever more radical and supportive of the communist political struggle.

"As a past Missionary in KwaZulu-Natal, Professor Beyerhaus was opposed to apartheid policy, but he also recognized that South Africa was one of the last strongholds of Christianity and that it was in danger of being destroyed in the interest of the New World Order. We are thankful that he gave us an insight into the *theology of liberation* which in essence is Marxist and atheistic. His books, *Violence in Jesus' Name.* (*Gewalt in Jesu Namen*), *The Uprising of the Poor* (*Aufbruch der Armen*) and *Theology as an*

Instrument of Liberation, together with many other interesting lectures, helped us to understand the church-political situation and allowed us to Biblically fight the good fight of Faith. Hence, Prof Beyerhaus contributed much to peace and goodwill.

"We thank God for the energy and dedication with which he brought the Word of God to South Africa with all its blessings. We praise the Lord who gave him such clear vision, wisdom and Spirit. A great man has passed away, who found his strength in Jesus Christ, for his testimony was: ***"I am not ashamed of the Gospel of Christ: for it is the power of God unto salvation to everyone that believeth."*** Romans 1:18."

This tribute corroborates what Frits Albers wrote in 1976 in the present work "The Beyerhaus Effect". It corroborates what he wrote in the recent newly published edition of his 1991 "The World Council of Churches" (En Route Books and Media, 2026) to which he closely tied the present book.

The tribute is a fitting preface to the present work of Frits Albers and his study of Prof. Beyerhaus' book "Bangkok '73", the profound insights he comes to light with and the conclusions he draws from them.

To understand what Frits Albers means by the 'Beyerhaus Effect' study this little, but very informative book. You will see what happens when orthodox Catholicism is introduced into ostensibly 'catholic' gatherings (lectures, seminars, courses, group discussions, retreats, pastoral councils etc, etc) planned (contrived) and controlled by Modernists and dissenters from Catholic Teaching; and most importantly, you will understand why it happens.

Introduction

For some years now, many good catholics: Priests, Nuns and Brothers, laypeople of all walks of life, have become painfully aware that, if questions of Orthodoxy, Papal Teaching, sound Catechetics and in general Catholic Church Doctrine are being introduced by them in all sorts of ostensibly 'catholic' gatherings: seminars, 'retreats', discussion groups, parent-teacher nights, pastoral councils, the reaction of the majority present is one of irritation, ridicule, impatience and other signs of intolerant hostility.

Baffled by these symptoms of rejection, and quite often unsure of themselves, their environment, and the origin of what is being presented, these good catholics have more and more taken refuge in the quiet decision of no longer attending such gatherings, for their own peace of mind and from the all-too-understandable feeling of 'What is the good'.

And yet they, not the others, are the bearers of the uninterrupted Apostolic Tradition living in the Catholic Church alone. They, not the others, have the right to be heard. They, not the others, are the salt of the earth, the light of the world, the yeast which is to go through the whole mixture.

Much of what I have written in the past has been to draw the attention to the origin, nature, symptoms and consequences of the 'hidden schism', which is leading millions of catholics on the road to the one – World 'church' of darkness, which His Holiness Pope St. Pius X foresaw as a consequence of the rampant modernism of his days, and of the 'great apostasy' which he saw at work in every country, according to his own testimony, in the world of his own time.

Armed with this information I hope that whoever read my documentations would find great consolation in increasing their love for Our Lady, for our Holy Mother the Catholic Church and for the priceless gift of their own Catholic Faith.

Yet more is required, so that these three great loves are introduced in the very gatherings and centres where they experience rejection. Heresy has no rights, least of all the right to be left alone. Heretics by the fact that they are human beings, have rights. Heresy has none. Many catholics who have fallen victim (sometimes quite unwittingly) to modernism, teilhardism, marxism, existentialism and other radical positions incompatible with membership of the Catholic Church, have a RIGHT, to be shown up, to be revealed to themselves, to be tripped up over their beliefs.

The Jewish leaders at the time of Our Lord's Sacred Passion and Death, wanted the whole unpleasant business over and done with as quickly and quietly as possible. But that was not God's idea. Although He had allowed the perpetrators of the Evil some power over the Sacred Body of His only-begotten Son, He remained fully in charge of events and at every turn that the Divine Drama took, the participants were forced by Divine Will to reveal their innermost thoughts, and the most secret convictions and passions were thus laid bare, as the Holy Man Simeon had already foretold would happen.

The same is now witnessed during the sacred passion of the Bride of the Son of God, Our Holy Mother the Catholic Church. In all sorts of gatherings and schemes, the modernists and teilhardians, so firmly entrenched in their local positions of power, want the local disfiguration and mutation of the Catholic Church being taken care of as quickly and secretly as possible. But here again: their anonymity is not the Will of God. Again, they may have been given some power, in God's Inscrutable Providence, over the Mystical Body of His Son, but, once again, God still remains fully in charge of events and at every turn the hidden plans and dark intentions of the modernists are being revealed and laid bare. God loves the sinner. And this love requires that sinners are made fully aware of what they are doing, so that they can reflect over their actions, see them for what they are, and repent. And so the rejection of orthodox catholics, of Papal teaching, of Tradition and Church Doctrine must be made public by Catholics who love their Faith as much as they love the poor modernist who lost his. In bringing these hidden rejections into the open, orthodox catholics may no longer be capable of reversing the Passion of the Church, but through God's Infinite Mercy they become instrumental in making sure that this sacred passion is not lost on the teilhardians and marxists.

To my knowledge it was Prof. Dr. Peter BEYERHAUS, a Lutheran theologian from Germany, who first revealed to the world, in a systematic study, what EFFECT the introduction of orthodoxy and orthodox theology has on a gathering of ostensibly ordinary christians, but who are led by other 'christians' wholly committed to marxism and modernism. It is out of gratitude to this man's findings that I have given to this present study the title it now bears: The 'BEYERHAUS EFFECT'. As already stated, so many of our good and sound catholics are unsure of the 'spiritual fabric' of which not a few of the present-day catholic gatherings are composed. If they knew the true nature of this fabric, they would have no qualms in tearing it. They need some guidance in assessing the orthodoxy of what is being proposed at such gatherings, a 'test for subversion'. My first task, therefore, will be to let Dr. Beyerhaus describe for us the elements out of which subversion is being composed, how it is actually being dressed up as truth, and what other means are being used to make sure that this subversion is being accepted as truth. Once catholics are familiar with these procedures, and proceed to test them for their orthodoxy, a REACTION takes place. It is to this reaction that I have given the name of the title of this study. In the second chapter I will illustrate from a few examples how the 'BEYERHAUS EFFECT' revealed to orthodox catholics the true nature of the 'spiritual fabric' that was being woven in some typical Australian situations by people who have absolutely no intention of saving souls.

Chapter One

The Ingredients of 'Spiritual Marxism'

In 1974 there appeared on the world scene an English translation of an incredible German book, written by a Lutheran Doctor in Theology in 1973, which book dispelled any doubts many of us may still have had about the religious future of the world. The title of the book is "Bangkok '73", and its author Prof. Dr. Peter Beyerhaus. If anyone still needs convincing that Modernism is conceived in hell, this book will achieve that.

Dr. Peter Beyerhaus is one of that rare breed of international theologians wholly uncontaminated by modernism, and his book "Bangkok '73" is an eyewitness account of what actually happened at the Eighth Conference on World Mission, held at Bangkok in 1973, under the auspices of the World Council of Churches. The title for this World Conference on Missions was, significantly enough, SALVATION TODAY.

In the Preface to his book, Prof. Beyerhaus explains the grave reasons he had for writing the account of the events which took place at SAMUT PRAKAN, the isolated centre of the World Conference near Bangkok with the following words:

> "It is my concern to share with the reader a profound uneasiness about certain pervasive signs in the ecumenical event which could be of disastrous consequence for the future of Missions, for Christianity and probably even for all Mankind.

> "Beneath my uneasiness lies a fully positive desire: I want to give readers information and a theological interpretation about the World Conference in Bangkok that can equip them – precisely here in the face of THE ERROR AND DECEIVING FORCE OF THIS CONFERENCE – to see more clearly than ever before their own Biblically grounded responsibility for the spread of the Gospel in all the world."

Chapter One: The Ingredients of 'Spiritual Marxism'

Prof. Beyerhaus then goes on to state that the perversion of Truth which became manifest at Bangkok was no accident, that it is now established policy TO DRESS ERROR UP with biblical quotations, and that a third ingredient is now necessary at these conferences to obtain the desired effect. Here are his own words with which he described it:

> "This book is made up of two major parts. The first part offers a comprehensive and reflective description of my impressions of the World Conference. For this book I have taken pains to study thoroughly the literature on Bangkok that has subsequently come to my attention. At the same time, it is on the basis of a thorough study of the practice of **SENSITIVITY TRAINING** that I wish to establish my main thesis: the most important thing to grasp concerning the troubling events at Samut Prakan is, that the organisers were conducting an experiment in GROUP DYNAMICS. In my opinion this is the most important discovery I made during the conference.

> "The second part of the book provides detailed documentation for my second thesis: Bangkok's understanding of Salvation WAS NOT THE BIBLICAL ONE, but rather a syncretistic and socio-political one; and further, where the Bible was apparently used, Christian assertions were ideologically undermined."

So there is the mixture of Bangkok '73: perversion by error dressed up in respectable theological and biblical garb, and the most sophisticated brainwashing techniques used to make the uncommitted accept and agree. But what respectable theological garb can ever dress up error as truth? Only the 'theology' of the late Pierre TEILHARD DE CHARDIN, which has been made respectable through its acceptance by nearly all theologians of world standing IN DEFIANCE OF CHURCH TEACHING. Prof. Beyerhaus again:

> "The Mission of Jesus Christ is not served today by a passionate WILL-TO-ACTION (the teilhardian existential act, as we saw in a pre-

vious work, FA), that despises clear differences in DOCTRINE (Thomism, FA), or by an experience in Group Dynamics, sentimentally glossing over the contemporary crisis in **THEOLOGICAL FOUNDATIONS.** But these attitudes have been elevated to DOGMA under the current Geneva administration of the World Council of Churches. Christ's message requires much more then this: first and foremost a passionate wrestling for biblical truth. For this truth alone will make us, and those who hear our missionary message, free."[1]

Let us then briefly examine the three ingredients of the Bangkok Conference as they are proposed here by Prof. Beyerhaus: (1) the perversion of the truth: (2) this perversion presented as the new interpretation of the biblical truth of Salvation, i.e. presented as ANOTHER GOSPEL, which they hold up as the new gospel of Jesus Christ, (which His Ho-

---

[1] A catholic author would have added here: 'a passionate wrestling for the truth of the living Magisterium of the Church, the true interpretation of Tradition'.

liness Pope St. Pius X has pointed out as a most distinguishing mark of the One-World 'church of darkness'): and finally (3) the experiment in Group Dynamics, to 'forcibly bring about the acceptance of this perversion', (which COERCION) was also foreseen and predicted by His Holiness Pope St. Pius X as another mark of the same 'church'). All the time we are conscious of the fact that we are studying a PROTO-TYPE, which has multiplied itself a million times over since then.

I. The Perversion of the Truth

Prof. Beyerhaus gave the following heading to the first chapter of his book: 'WHAT IS MEANT BY "SALVATION" IN THE BANGKOK MOTTO "SALVATION TODAY"?'

> "The theme for the eighth conference on World Mission, 'SALVATION TODAY', was announced shortly after the General Assembly of the World Council of Churches (WCC) held at UPPSALA, Sweden, in 1968. How was the slogan chosen? The constitu-

Chapter One: The Ingredients of 'Spiritual Marxism'

tion of the Commission for World Mission and Evangelism of the WCC, established in NEW DELHI in 1961 and with which almost all national mission councils of the world are affiliated, states that its mandate is to work to further the proclamation to the whole world of the Gospel of Jesus Christ to the end that all men may believe in Him and be saved.

"Here as in the tradition of the international missions movement of the 18th and 19th centuries, 'salvation' bestowed on those who believe in the message of salvation proclaimed by Jesus Christ, was the goal. Our predecessors' understanding of this salvation, i.e. redemption or deliverance, was always unequivocal, because of their firm commitment to Holy Scripture. It was deliverance of sinners from the wrath of God, including both present reconstitution of fellowship with Him through the forgiveness of human guilt and also acquittal at the Judgement Day.

> "But just two years after accepting such a gratifying biblical statement of purpose, it became apparent that this very understanding of salvation was being called into question by the now ECUMENICALLY ALIGNED Mission Agencies."

Here Prof. Beyerhaus identifies the existence of a FALSE ECUMENISM and the basis of its programme: a RADICAL DEPARTURE from and BREAK WITH the biblical truth of salvation. He then proceeds to show how various conferences, starting with the Seventh World Conference in Mexico City in 1963, have severely questioned this concept of salvation.

> "This thinking broke out into open conflict five years later at UPPSALA, in the second session, whose assignment was to treat the subject 'RENEWAL IN MISSIONS', so-called horizontalists and verticalists, otherwise designated as ECUMENICALS and EVANGELICALS, suddenly emerged in open dispute .... Ecumenicals by contrast

Chapter One: The Ingredients of 'Spiritual Marxism'

> proclaimed HUMANIZATION so-called as the only sensible goal of missions today. Dialogue and also, in certain circumstances, participation in the revolutionary movements of our time, were said to mark the path of the goal. All these, it was stated, are likewise part of the MISSIO DEI, which goes far beyond the Church's traditional forms of outreach, that mission of God that is being worked out in world history. God can go – so it goes – 'beyond the church' to get His business done by using Marxists, humanists and members of other religions."

This severe polarisation had of course a reaction and serious minded scholars, concerned at the depth of feeling shown at Uppsala, set about to do some salutary soul searching.

> "When all is said and done, the issue dividing them was their fundamentally conflicting views on the nature of salvation. It became progressively clearer that ecumenically organised missions WERE IN THE THROES OF A

DEEP AND FUNDAMENTAL CRISIS OF THEOLOGY."

Providentially for us, Prof. Beyerhaus, with his reputation as an international scholar, did not leave us long in the dark about the aspects of this crisis in theology:

> "The most deceptive aspect of this crisis was that, although these novel ideas were expressed frankly in ideological terms, such as 'humanization', 'identity', 'dialogue', 'revolution', etc., they also, and much more importantly were expressed in a biblical phraseology, which, however, had been secretly given a totally different meaning."

From the words used here, carefully chosen by a scholar of international reputation: 'humanization', 'identity', the designated source of confusion points unmistakably, once again, to TEILHARD DE CHARDIN. And the other words, equally carefully chosen: 'revolution', point to the use that is being made of this teilhardian confusion: MARXISM. I

Chapter One: The Ingredients of 'Spiritual Marxism'

once again remind the reader here, that it was His Holiness Pope Pius XII, who in his encyclical *Humani Generis* categorically declared that the aberrations caused by evolution (teilhardism) would advance the cause of communism. Now, if this was only a confusion in theology, bad as it was, it would not necessarily be catastrophic. But there is much more involved.

> "In this confusion we certainly see the profoundest source of the tragedy at Bangkok, and indeed in the ecumenical movement altogether. And the SPIRITUAL ERROR AND CONFUSION OF THE ECUMENICAL MOVEMENT arose in turn from the fundamental crisis in the view of Scripture, found in the theology of the member churches."

This really means that Prof. Beyerhaus is now also pointing the finger at a CRISIS IN FAITH, because it is in FAITH that we accept the Word of God written in Scripture. And this of course is serious. He continues:

"The preliminary investigation of the theme SALVATION TODAY was to have constructed a bridge on the twin piles of SCRIPTURE and the contemporary situation, that is, EXPERIENCE. (Advocates of the LIFE SITUATION METHOD, please sit up and take note! FA). Needless to say, difficulties which had not been anticipated quickly appeared to hamper the project. THE TWO SIDES OF THE EQUATION, proposed in the formula 'SCRIPTURE AND EXPERIENCE' REFUSED TO ADMIT EQUALITY. It now seems less and less probable that an ecumenical consensus will be reached by the help of such a study. Ecumenical pluralism, revealed here as a CRIPPLING INFLUENCE on theology, affected first the exegetical studies of the concept of salvation."

So the H.Q. of the WCC in Geneva had a veritable 'Babel of confusion' on its hands, and somehow, if the Bangkok Conference was to take place at all, the organizers had to make a decision and opt for something. In the description that follows it will be almost impossible to imagine how a supposedly responsible organisation could have made such a fatal decision in the most crucial part of its history. IT TOO, IN THE WORDS OF POPE ST. PIUS X:

> "has been harnessed in its course by the MODERN enemies of the Church, and it (too) is now no more than a miserable effluent of the great movement of apostasy, being organized in every country for the establishment of the ONE-WORLD 'church' ..." (*Our Apostolic Mandate*, 1910).

For here is how Prof. Beyerhaus describes this capitulation:

> "If it is now asked where the interests of the MAJORITY of the Geneva staff directly responsible for conference planning lay, and what position its ecumenical confidants all over the world maintained, it must be answered that they have to be classed in essentials with the group caring so much about

the longing for **SECULAR SALVATION TODAY**."

This means, according to the Professor, that the true meaning of the slogan 'SALVATION TODAY' has been decided by the Geneva planners as being 'SECULAR SALVATION TODAY'. Prof. Beyerhaus substantiates his conclusion with these words:

> "Two observations made this evident to me. The FIRST came from listening to a tape from Geneva, containing a discussion on 'SALVATION TODAY' by the chief representatives of the Ecumenical Commission on World Mission and Evangelism (CWME). In this discussion the concept of salvation was discussed in its linguistic, political and social aspects, as well as in terms of the history of religions. NONE OF THE PARTICIPANTS in the discussion by even a single word expressed awareness of the fact, that in the biblical sense, salvation is first of all the RECONCILIATION OF THE SINNER WITH GOD on the basis of the sin-

Chapter One: The Ingredients of 'Spiritual Marxism'

offering of Jesus Christ. Instead such revealing comments as the following were spoken:

> 'In Latin America young people begin to see Che Guevara and Jesus Christ as belonging to the same tradition ...'

A book that appeared in February 1972 under the title 'SALVATON TODAY AND CONTEMPORARY EXPERIENCE' gave me my SECOND opportunity to discover the peculiarly Genevan understanding of salvation. This book is a collection of excerpts from contemporary works in the fields of politics, pop music, modern literature, Marxist philosophy, and even radical theology. These were said to articulate modern man's concern for salvation. One of these testimonies is the report of a Red Chinese under the title 'Saved by Man'. Even more shocking is the concluding piece, 'The Priest and the Apostate', taken from a contemporary Japanese novel 'SILENCE'. This contribution contends that denial of belief in Christ for the sake of fellow prisoners during a time of persecution is a realization of SALVATION TODAY! This volume was the MAJOR PREPARATORY DOCUMENT FOR BANGKOK and was especially recommended as such by the officials of the Department for World Mission and Evangelism (DWME)."

One objection raised against this formulation of the agenda for Bangkok came from a Norway delegate, who expressed himself in these words:

"Salvation then appears to be the answer to man's longing for welfare, peace, liberty and happiness. Salvation is then more accurately described as 'solution'."

But if that is the way to decide the approach to the problem of salvation, then the slogan coined by Werner Simpendorfer as quoted by Prof. Beyerhaus:

> "The WORLD determines the Church's agenda."

takes on the precise meaning of Teilhard's axiom:

> "What increasingly dominates my interests is the effort to establish within myself and to diffuse around me A NEW RELIGION, AS THE CULTURAL AND RELIGIOUS STAGE WE HAVE REACHED NOW DEMANDS."

Which means we have now come full circle. For it was TEILHARD who gave to marxist evolutionism its MYSTIQUE, its armchair ride to god-omega, which is now being used by the Marxists to proclaim the secular salvation: 'the great apostasy'. As long as teilhardian evolution is the basis of catechetics, theology, seminary training and all sorts of conferences, seminars and 'retreats': SPIRITUAL MARXISM is not only SAFE: IT IS INEVITABLE ...

And so the 'delicate fabric' to be woven on this prototype of all perversion: the Bangkok Conference, was going to be officially: 'Spiritual Marxism. But in order to achieve the objective and to prevent the rending, COERCION of the most sophisticated type was going to be employed, the duplication of which in millions of other 'situations' has become the beginning of the great persecution of the great bulk of silent, orthodox, faithful catholics, whose simple other-worldly Faith is being ridiculed by the satanic marxist 'catholics' constantly (mis)quoting from 'THE DOCUMENTS OF VATICAN II'.

But God would not be God, if His faithful servants were not in possession of the ultimate weapon ...

So far we have analysed that a powerful body of very intelligent men, world-leaders in the 'christian' faith, has made the decision (1) that the time has come that the Gospel of Our Lord regarding Salvation and Redemption is to be radically changed and (2) that a World Conference on Salvation is going to adopt this perversion and (3) that the 'spiritual fabric' of the World Conference is going to be permeated with this new spiritual marxism.

Catholics the world over have by now ceased to wonder if such attempts were effectively barred from having any influence at all over catholics. The strong words of our present Holy Father: 'The smoke of Satan is seeping into the Church through the cracks', and the earlier testimony of Pope St. Pius X: 'The poison is diffused through the whole tree, in the very heart and veins of the Church, SO THAT THERE IS NO PART OF CATHOLIC TRUTH WHICH THEY LEAVE UNTOUCHED, NONE THAT THEY DO NOT STRIVE TO CORRUPT', testify to a very serious situation. In fact, the reverse question is far more pertinent nowadays: 'One wonders if the teaching of Our Lord and His Vicar on earth have still any effect at all on the majority of catholics ...' And so the determined attempts to subversion described so far by Prof. Beyerhaus, have according to the Popes of our times, A DIRECT BEARING on the catholic situation.

Catholics must acquaint themselves with the description Prof. Beyerhaus gives to this subversion, not only to recognise it when they come face to face with it, but also, far from being impressed by it, to have no qualms in resisting it and tearing the fabric thus created.

Let us now proceed to inform ourselves how, according to Prof. Beyerhaus, this satanic effluent was being dressed up and presented as the gospel of Jesus Christ and how BIBLICAL TEACHING had to be perverted in order to achieve this. Catholics can and must extend this to mean, in their own situation, how CATHOLIC TEACHING has been twisted and bent and especially the teachings of the Second Vatican Council.

II. The New 'Biblical Truth' of Salvation

In order that such a radically different concept of salvation can have any hope of being accepted by a large body of believers at such an important gathering as a World Conference on Missions, it is necessary to either 'convert' every participant to humanism, or else convince him that his biblical convictions are outdated, and that the modern interpretations of Scripture can now accommodate these concepts. The second approach is far superior to the first one. It had shown its worth through the use IDOC made of it in its process of 'updating' many 'backward' Bishops prior to their full participation in the deliberations during the Second Vatican Council. It is still very successfully made use of in all sorts of seminaries, seminars, deep-sharing weekends and so-called retreats to wean catholics away from their Catholic Faith. The 'drawback' of course is that such a technique has to be used since this training in apostasy cannot be left to Heaven, no matter how much or how often the Holy Ghost is being mentioned by these perpetrators.

The fundamental aspect of all such techniques is the devilish subtle appeal to one's aversion from ridicule and rejection, which makes all sensitivity training and group dynamics courses so highly successful. Leaving this latter aspect to the next (third) subsection let us concentrate here on how the biblical understanding was 'enlarged' to accommodate the modern interpretations of salvation, which the organisers had decided was the one to be presented at the Bangkok Conference, and which they were determined to have accepted there AS BIBLICAL ...

"The Geneva HQ apparently did not realize that, where this issue was concerned, it had not so much run into difficulty inherent to the matter under consideration, but that it had instead blundered into the undertow of the fundamental crisis in modern exegesis", says Prof. Beyerhaus, after which he proceeds to list five (5) observations one ecumenical institute had sent to Geneva, which observations he considered important as manifestations of the contemporary attitude to the Bible held by ecumenical theology.

(a) "The Bible is only human testimony to the Revelation of God, but not the binding thrust of the Revelation itself.

(b) The great variety of biblical writings, sources and editorial levels allow these human testimonies concerning God's Revelation to appear contradictory to each other.

(c) A contemporary salvation experience, or an expectation of salvation, can be regarded as biblical based, if it conforms to ANY historical experience of the old covenant people, e.g. the political exodus-motif, even if such a political event cannot be established as a Christian experience of salvation from the standpoint of the New Testament. (This line of thought was prominent in the use of the Bible at Bangkok).

Chapter One: The Ingredients of 'Spiritual Marxism'

(d) The Bible does not provide us with an eternally valid picture of the salvation message, but only with a series of translations which have been adjusted to the time-bound notions and variable circumstances of the people who have heard and read the message. Biblical passages, therefore, can be made meaningful only if they are translated anew in the light of our modern conditions. These translations transform not only the form of the language, but even the content itself so that it too can be experienced as (biblical) salvation.

(e) The Bible's testimony to revelation is not on an essentially different level than testimonies to the saving work of the same God outside the biblical history of election and in Christian history after the biblical era."

'Fear' was held that division between Revelation and Scripture was too stark to be presented as such to the Conference, and that it would not go down well with many delegates, unfamiliar with this form of DIALECTIC 'Theology'. A principle had to be found which would unite all these apparently disharmonious statements. Wieser finally discovered this principle in the pietistic concept of the 'witness'. A witness is not expected to reflect dogmatic clarity but only the genuineness of his own actual EXPERIENCE of salvation.

"How biblically Christian is this?"

This was never answered. ... The question of course answers itself: Revelation and Holy Scripture were never subject to PERSONAL EXPERIENCE, which is nothing but a form of existentialism with its total rejection of any outside norm or criterium.

III. The Experiment in Group Dynamics

From what has been gathered so far it has become abundantly clear, that a Thomistic search for the Nature and Truth of things before any intellectual assent could be given, would under the circumstances be definitely out. This priceless DISCIPLINE OF THE MIND, the only true basis for any

Chapter One: The Ingredients of 'Spiritual Marxism'

Supernatural Reality, would not be allowed to be used to form an intelligent, rational basis for any missionary action. If you are tied up with a group of revolutionaries, who want to use the Church and the Bible TO FURTHER THE ENDS OF MARXISM, the last thing these people allow you to do is to find out about them and their plans, and to come to light with the TRUTH of the situation. This required considerable skill from the plotters on two quite distinct levels.

1. To let the sound theology and theological debate vanish without its absence being noticed, and
2. to get a broad consensus on the marxist-revolutionary idea of salvation.

According to Prof. Beyerhaus, they succeeded only too well on both counts. This is what he had to say:

"The division of the Bangkok Conference into its 3 Sections corresponded to the three-pronged attack on Orthodoxy from the point of view of the ecumenical concern: (1) Culture and Identity: (2) Salvation and Social Justice: (3) Church Renewal through Mission.

"Given such a programming of the conference, so clearly obvious even in the process of preparation, an earnest theological effort by all participants for an exegetical and doctrinal clarification of the central theme 'SALVATION TODAY', could only function AS A BREAK OR DESTRUCTIVE FORCE. Therefore, an entirely different means had to be chosen to reach the goal: the theological study material, gathered for a period of three years, was simply allowed to disappear from sight, and in its place the delegates to Bangkok were summoned to 'AN EXPERIMENT IN GROUP DYNAMICS'."

So the delegates knew beforehand. Prof. Beyerhaus made that quite clear. The plotters had to show their hand in order to forestall any objections to the frustration of any orthodox approach and to the disappearance of any orthodox study material. But apparently not knowing what to expect, it appeared that the delegates were prepared to co-operate, and so the advanced warning worked in favour of the organisers.

I would like to draw the attention of the reader to the words of Prof. Beyerhaus quoted above, indicating the EFFECT the introduction of orthodoxy and orthodox (Thomistic) theology has on this sort of marxist MEDIUM. I have made this effect the title of this study. The Prof. will come back to this phenomenon later on in his book, when we will be in a better position to come to the conclusion that, if the introduction of orthodoxy and orthodox theology, and the discipline of the mind, has a BRAKING or TEARING EFFECT, the MEDIUM (or so-called 'spirituality') in which it is introduced, is MARXIST and anti-God.

Let us return to the narrative of Prof. Beyerhaus, where he tells us how it came about that the advanced warning worked in favour of the organisers.

"Early in December 1972, Dr Gerhard Hoffman, the former executive secretary of the German Protestant Missionary Council, who had just taken a position at the Geneva HQ of the CWME, sent a reply to Pastor P. G. Buttler, his successor in Hamburg. Pastor Buttler had posed a question concerning the preparatory theological documents for Bangkok. Dr. Hoffman replied to his letter as follows:

> 'The group leaders are not tied to definite texts. They can come with their own preparation, but they must face the insights of others who find other texts OR INTERPRETATIONS (Vatican II, for Catholic readers! FA.) more important. For the other groups too something analogous applies. Preparation is not possible on a mere intellectual level, BUT RATHER BY BEING TUNED INTO A THEME. This does not exclude an intellectual German theological discussion, but it reduces the possibility to a contribution. As you stated: the

German delegation is crying out for preparatory material. The first answer therefore would be: DO NOT BLOCK YOURSELVES AGAINST AN EXPERIMENT IN GROUP DYNAMICS, and still less AGAINST THE MOVING OF GOD'S SPIRIT, which is at least possible. Rather prepare yourselves in a different way this time. Is it not 'preparation' if somebody somewhere discovers a new song, contemplates on it, and takes it along to Bangkok? Of course he may also bring along biblical texts which have just become important to him'." (End of quoted part of letter.)

Prof. Beyerhaus continues:

"Owing to its apparent originality, this plan surprised a good number of delegates and encouraged them to open themselves up for the experiment. But responsible, thinking participants felt themselves frustrated at

Bangkok. 'This is the most boring congress I have ever participated in' one American delegate was heard to remark. He had, of course, not perceived that the boredom could be a direct design of the guidelines governing such an experiment in Group Dynamics.[2]"

Prof. Beyerhaus then introduces Group Dynamics to his readers. He says that the tactics of group dynamics and its twin 'sensitivity training' are well known and are available to whoever is interested in finding out for himself.

E.g. the experimenters will not give you an agenda until the very last minute. They will make a big display of allowing something to take place which the victims would consider important, but they sandwich it so, that it becomes immediately nullified. By the time enough delegates are organised to

---

[2] At the end of this chapter, I will refer back to this passage: 'of opening themselves up', and, in the words of Prof. Beyerhaus, draw the final, inevitable conclusion, 'what they really opened themselves up to at this Conference in Bangkok'.

Chapter One: The Ingredients of 'Spiritual Marxism'   41

do something about it, the moment, opportunity and effect have passed because of a 'tight schedule to be kept'. They are always very polite and apologetic about that: the more frustrated you get, the more it plays into their scheme to single you out and isolate you. Under no circumstance will the conference be allowed to choose its own format or schedule: the iron-clad fist which runs the show is masked by flowers, soft lights, dances, holding hands, sing-songs and the like. Prof. Beyerhaus:

> "The Conference schedule, which was released only at the beginning, provided space for just a few public addresses and still fewer opportunities to discuss them. Actually, the Geneva establishment itself was the only voice heard from the podium. The only lecture touching on fundamental theology was sandwiched between two reports. ... Even a first, dispassionate readings of some of the Bangkok findings and resolutions as reported by the press, took the breath away from non-participants. The call for a temporary suspension (or moratorium) on the sending

of further missionaries, and the China resolution were particularly shocking. The burning question arises immediately: 'How could these recommendations be composed without the presence of any dissent or even a minority opinion (both in the conference and in the smaller General Assembly of the CWME following it immediately) WHEN BOTH GROUPS WERE SO THOROUGHLY DIVIDED?' What actually was the method used? In the letter cited above from Geneva to Hamburg, Dr. Gerhard Hoffman had called the method planned for Bangkok AN EXPERIMENT IN GROUP DYNAMICS. Such experiments seek to create a specific psychological climate within a group of all sorts of people; and in this group all participants, IN SPITE OF THEIR ORIGINAL RESISTANCE, are finally brought into a united community of emotions, thought and will. The Geneva officials, who desired the effect of this mass-psychological movement, sought to relate it to the MOVEMENT OF THE SPIRIT OF GOD."

Chapter One: The Ingredients of 'Spiritual Marxism'   43

We are rapidly coming to the heart of the matter. If 326 serious, Mission-minded delegates come together to study the ADVANCE of global missionary activity, and then come out with the exact opposite: calling for a HALT, a MORATORIUM on missionary activity, thinking honestly they were doing God and the missions a good turn. Then who on earth can guarantee that ANYONE will come out of such an experiment, thinking the same, believing the same that he believed when he went in. He can only be sure of one thing: HE WILL BE MADE TO BELIEVE THE OPPOSITE, STILL THINKING IT IS THE SAME ... How is that done?

> "THE TRUE KEY TO UNDERSTANDING AND PLANNNG OF THE COURSE OF THE BANGKOK CONFERENCE LIES IN THE PROFESSED **EQUATION** BETWEEN A SYSTEMATICALLY STAGED SOCIO-PSYCHOLOGICAL EXPERIMENT AND THE ACTION OF THE HOLY SPIRIT."

And Prof. Beyerhaus then sets out, in a packed 22 pages, to show from every angle and with a welter of detail, how this perversion OF EQUATING BRAINWASHING WITH THE HOLY SPIRIT was carried out. Nothing was left to chance. Even the objection that such an exercise is impossible is squarely met. The poor delegates did not have a chance from the word go. [And judging by the innumerable catholics who now believe the opposite of what the Church taught us before, who no longer can tell the difference between Catholic Faith and Christian Faith, and who think that 'being on the pill' and 'Humanae Vitae' can go together: the experiment did not stop at Bangkok, but has swept the world.] The whole matter is so important, and it touches so centrally on the problem of our times, that we will stay a little longer with Prof. Beyerhaus for further enlightenment.

He starts on very solid ground by quoting from the most authoritative book so far on the subject of Group Dynamics and Sensitivity Training: "BEYOND WORDS: THE STORY OF SENSITIVITY TRAINING AND THE ENCOUNTER MOVEMENT", by Kurt W. Back (New York, 1972) from which are quoted all the relevant particulars such as:

(1) "There is a wealth of workshops, laboratories, educational schemes, books and tapes in which the methods of Sensitivity Training are more thoroughly developed, and which have been placed at the disposal of scientists, psychotherapists, politicians, private persons, AND NOW EVEN ECCLESIASTICAL AUTHORITIES, PARTICULARLY ECUMENICAL OFFICIALS."

(2) "Sensitivity Training has two critical essential features: (a) it gives its participants a tremendous emotional experience, that they can even sometimes describe as a new birth (as in the charismatic renewal); and (b) it is considered by its advocates as an invaluable means to alter people inwardly, and thereby to make them better members of their group and better listeners to it. Of particular note in this is, that S.T. has had religious undertones since its beginning. It has assumed the function OF PROVIDING A CONSISTENT WORLD-VIEW

WHICH COINCIDES WITH ECUMENISM. IT IS THE MOST IMPORTANT TOOL FOR THE ECUMENICAL MOVEMENT ..."

So far the quote from Back. Prof. Beyerhaus then remarks "So much for the 'action of the Holy Spirit' ...". And he is true. This false ecumenism which is sweeping the world, uncritically hailed by Nuns, Priests, Brothers, Bishops and Catholic laypeople alike, although it requires the suppression BY CATHOLICS of a DOGMA OF THE CATHOLIC FAITH: 'that the Catholic Church is the ONE, TRUE CHURCH founded by Christ for the spiritual salvation of the world': such an utterly false ecumenism cannot come from the Holy Spirit, and therefore can only lead to the one-world 'church of darkness'. As predicted by Pope St. Pius X in his encyclical *Our Apostolic Mandate*. A movement which EQUATES its activities with the activity of the Holy Spirit, yet professes to be in need of the most ultramodern and refined methods of brainwashing techniques known to further its ends and obtain its objectives, exposes itself AS A FRAUD and not coming from the Holy Spirit at all. This, as we will see, was my FUNDAMENTAL OBJECTION to the preparation of the First National Conference of Catholic Laity in Australia, held in Sydney in April, 1976. The same IRON FIST of Marxism was there under the constant invocation of the Holy Spirit ...

Prof. Beyerhaus then takes us through all the aspects of how these basic rules were applied at Bangkok. Of great importance is the COMPLETE MUTUAL OPENESS, so that people can expose their vulnerability. He quotes Dr. Hoffman in an interview for the South West German Radio:

> "We hope that there are enough people here who are vulnerable, and who will let themselves be wounded, so that they can hear the strange things and the unheard of things which have never yet been heard that others will say to them ..."

And Prof. Beyerhaus' comment:

> "This meant that we should be ready to call all the convictions in question, and all the

presuppositions we brought with us, and even that we should abandon them in order to open ourselves up to the 'unheard of things', perhaps even that which CONTRADICTS OUR CHRISTIAN FAITH.

"The Conference wanted to achieve one objective: to involve its participants in the **ecumenical socio-political movement**. For the success of a new social movement, according to the American sociologist H. Blumer, four fundamental factors are important:

> *First*, a **general uneasiness** in which men are responsive to a new appeal;
> *Second*, a **popular rising**, in which all are agreed as to the sources of the difficulty and in which the goals of the movement are clearly defined;
> *Third*, **indoctrination**, i.e. the creation of a body of dogmas and a vanguard of adherents to disseminate them; and

Fourth, **institutionalization** which is necessary in order to realize the goals of the movement."

WE COULD NOT WISH FOR A BETTER BIRTH CERTIFICATE OF THE EXPECTED ONE-WORLD CHURCH OF DARKNESS.

- **EVOLUTION** has created a world-wide *uneasiness* with regard to Christianity and especially with regard to the Catholic Church in Her prohibitions against Teilhard de Chardin.
- **ECUMENISM** has become *the popular uprising* in which all are asked to agree that 'the old Church' is the source of the difficulty. The Catholic Church with Her claim to UNIQUENESS has kept us all divided.
- **GROUP DYNAMICS** with sensitivity training as its most potent ingredient will release these pent-up feelings (charismatic renewal, and such) and will consolidate these vague notions into dogmas by indoctrination.

- **ONE-WORLD CHURCH** of Ecumenism and Unity will *institutionalize* it all on a world wide scale in the name of the World Council of Churches and the Holy Spirit ...

And then we are ready for anti-christ. And the point of crystallisation, around which it all falls into place, is TEILHARD DE CHARDIN, who made evolution and evolutionary theology into 'MYSTIQUE'. From now on we can be sure that ALL world-congresses will be run along the lines of the Bangkok sensitivity training experiment TO FURTHER THE CAUSE OF MARXISM. Liberation theology, Teilhardian teaching and group dynamics are the loom on which the 'spiritual' marxism will be woven until such time that the 'church of darkness' can afford to scotch the pretence and will show itself in all its ugliness ... 'for the oppression of the weak, and all those who toil and suffer' predicted by Pope St. Pius X. Let us listen a bit longer to Prof. Beyerhaus:

"Through the method used at the Conference, group processes were set in motion, which compelled the individual to speak and listen EXISTENTIALLY, and in this atmosphere of interpersonal encounter all efforts to construct abstract and systematic theology (Thomism) seemed almost IN-HUMAN and certainly UN-CHRISTIAN."

Another reference by the author to the Beyerhaus Effect.

"The import of the Bangkok SECTION REPORTS is only fully revealed when some acquaintance has been gained with the IDEOLOGICAL forms of Sensitivity Training, especially as they have been developed in the USA. The Ecumenical Institute in Chicago deserves special mention. Its influence is spread OVER ALL THE WORLD through a network of daughter institutions. The important thing to note in these reports IS THE NEW INTER-PRETATION OF CHRISTIAN TALK, underpinned as it is by another ideology. These reports sketch the blurred contours of AN APPROACHING

UNIFIED RELIGION (unmistakable reference to the prophecy of Pope St. Pius X about an approaching 'church of darkness') in which christianity contributes merely some formal suggestions for the general ideas of God and salvation. The name of Christ is still retained, BUT IN THE SENSE OF THE **COSMIC CHRISTOLOGY** PROMULGATED AT NEW DELHI."

Has ever the 'church of darkness' been better identified with TEILHARD DE CHARDIN, than here by this non-Catholic research theologian? The false ecumenism sweeping the world is NOT to bring unity around the Son of Mary, but around the figment of a teilhardian imagination under the slavery of Communism. The same Pope who predicted:

"The world might well be united, but only in a common ruin".

was also the one who predicted that the aberrations of (teilhardian) evolution WOULD ADVANCE

THE CAUSE OF COMMUNISM. (Pope Pius XII. *Humani Generis.* 1950).

Prof. Beyerhaus continues:

"There are others who think that it is a good idea for Sensitivity Training to be introduced into the many phases of the established German churches, as for example the Protestant Academies. I do not think that this evaluation is justified. For Sensitivity Training always leads to a change in personality. LIKE SO-CALLED CHARISMATIC RENEWAL, it makes people WEAK IN THEIR CHARACTERS AND SPIRITS, unable to resist dangerous influences by destroying the protective layers of normal social behavior. By these unprincipled means many people in different places HAVE BEEN PROGRAMMED INTO ACCEPTING THE COMMON MORALITY, THE COMMON WORLDVIEW and the ideological code-words of a particular group. Such 'sensitised' people have lost the individuality which God has given them. As a consequence, such people will let themselves be swept along by any movement capturing the loyalty of the group: they are the ones who will go along willingly should a Fuhrer (antichrist!) gifted with demonic charisma, establish himself as the dictator of a society prepared by such training."

These clear words underscore two observations made by St. John, under Divine inspiration, in the Apocalypse: (a) that it will be a **religious leader** who will introduce Anti-christ to the world, and (b) THAT THE WHOLE WORLD will run after the Beast.

Prof. Beyerhaus:

"As christians we should use our spiritual insights to assess these novel characteristics of the modern ecumenical movement. We should make it clear that WHERE ANOTHER JESUS IS PROCLAIMED BY ANOTHER GOSPEL, ANOTHER SPIRIT IS ALSO

PRESENT THERE (2 Cor. 11:4). For the problem of a dialogue amounts to becoming sensitive to the work of the Holy Spirit in the world and that, to be sure, not only within religions, but also within the beliefs and ideologies of THIS WORLD. The ecumenical education programme of education has here, it seems to me, betrayed (revealed) its most precipitous aspect: the goal is to make the christian SENSITIVE for a work of the Spirit in the very place where, according to Holy Scripture HE IS NEVER AT WORK (2 Cor. 6:14). The serious question arises from this as to what spirit christians are really opening themselves up to when they enter into this programme designed to improve their sensitivity."

This warning of Prof. Beyerhaus is timely. The Holy Spirit is never at work in deceit, lying, brainwashing and all the other activities of false ecumenism. To allow a false replica of ecumenism to spread unopposed for fear of offending the Holy Spirit if it was counteracted, is blasphemy.

And what DID St. Paul say in 2 Cor. 6:14-17?

"Do not harness yourselves in an uneven team with unbelievers. Virtue is no companion for crime. LIGHT AND DARKNESS HAVE NOTHING IN COMMON. Christ is not the ally of Beliar, NOR HAS A BELIEVER ANYTHING TO SHARE WITH AN UNBELIEVER. The temple of God has no common ground with idols. And that is what we are, the temple of the living God: we have God's word for that: 'I will make my home among them and will live among them. I will be their God, and they will be my people. THEN COME AWAY FROM THEM, AND KEEP ALOOF, says the Lord. Touch nothing that is unclean and I will welcome you and be your Father, and you shall be my sons and daughters, says the Almighty Lord'."

Chapter Two

The Detection and Destruction of 'Spiritual Marxism'

If I dwelt on the subject-matter of the previous chapter in such detail, consider it as a matter of 'have to', because so many good catholics are as much in the dark about the enemy and his tactics as they are ignorant of the clear teaching of the Church. They either mistrust all changes and suffer needlessly, or else they just go along with everything and do not suffer enough. Many just keep to themselves, having lost all missionary incentive, leaving all others to God; others have become impressed by the claims of the false ecumenism 'that everybody goes to heaven by his own road', which means there is no longer any need for missionary zeal, since one road is as good as another. One way everything is left to God, out of 'Quietism' and 'Pietism', condemned by the Church, the other way everything is left to the Devil, because a personal or local 'moratorium on missionary activity' has been adopted for exactly the same reason as it was adopted at Bangkok. Either way the noisy demand by the false ecumenism: 'that Catholics play down their claim on a unique Church' out of 'charity and consideration for their fellow christians' has had a paralysing effect all around, and every day we are vividly reminded of the dire complaint spoken by Our Lady at FATIMA:

> "Many souls go to hell because no one prays or makes sacrifices for them".

And so the most salutary shock to the system for many would be the realisation that there is a war on, and that this war can and must be won. If the first chapter familiarised us with the enemy and his tactics, then this one must equip us with the means to seek him out and pursue him. For he is very elusive and appears under many guises, but mostly (as St. Paul assures us) 'as an angel of light' (2 Cor. 11:14). As stated in the beginning of this study on subversion: it is quite possibly too late by now that the tide can be reversed, and so it may well be, that the Catholic Church will have to go to Her own Calvary

Chapter Two: The Detection and Destruction of 'SM'   59

in the most terrible persecutions yet to be unleashed. But the enemy is still subject to God's Sovereignty AND MUST BE EXPOSED AT EVERY TURN OF THE PASSION OF THE CHURCH. And it is precisely here, in the area of unmasking, that the 'BEYERHAUS EFFECT' gives us invaluable assistance.

We saw that Prof. Beyerhaus accurately observed that the introduction of orthodoxy, or orthodox theology, into the 'climate' created by the Bangkok planners, would have the most startling effects. Words used by him were: 'braking', 'destructive force', 'inhuman' and 'non-christian'. Now it is beyond a shadow of a doubt, that, if orthodoxy was made to come in contact with a climate created by the Holy Spirit no such effects would be produced. The violent reaction only results if the 'fruits of the Holy Spirit' are brought in contact with 'the poison of teilhardism or marxism'. Many, many catholics in the past have suffered from the rejection symptoms which are associated with the 'Beyerhaus effect', WITHOUT PURSUING THE MATTER ANY FURTHER because they did not understand. But if the effect is deliberately produced by catholics who know what they are about, the resulting exposure of Satan beneath the disguise of the angel of light is quite shattering for the perpetrators of the fraud. They may not abandon their evil attempts for power through the Sacred, but they certainly experience what Prof. Beyerhaus called a 'braking force': they are slowed down. They are forced to reveal their thoughts and intentions, and in many ways they are forced to do their dirty work more openly, so that other catholics may become aware of what goes on and are given a chance to make up their minds. We may accept the fact that the Church too is destined to 'empty Herself' for the sake of a sinful humanity, but Her Dignity and Honour are still very much OUR CONCERN. That, and the fact that we are brothers' keepers, and this love for our brothers requires that they become aware of what they are doing, even if it is through OUR USE OF THE BEYERHAUS EFFECT. I will now, by means of a few examples, show how this effect can reveal a hostile environment, and what ought to be done, once such a situation has come to light.

(A) The Catechesis Syndrome

In 1972 I had reason to submit to ROME a well-documented dossier on how Catholic Truth was being mutilated, distorted and suppressed in the Archdiocese of Melbourne. From this folder I select the following item exactly as it was submitted. In 1971 I had joined a Catechetics Formation Course to get first hand knowledge of what was being taught and the following item was the first lecture, opening the 1972 series. General heading: 'CHRISTIAN FORMATION LECTURES: sub-heading: 'EDUCATION IN FAITH'. The 'notes' were nothing but about twenty lines, spread out over a foolscap sheet. In it we were taught that faith is:

> "**Christian** faith is a person's acceptance of God's self-revelation. It is a personal knowledge of God, of his loving design, of his will to save men."

And at the end we are told:

> "The community of faith is united in worship. Worship-Eucharist the centre of all **Christian** Life."

It was nothing but the by now usual double-talk. I now quote from my comment to Rome:

> "After this first lecture on the first night, I asked the lecturing Priest: 'This is all very well, Father, but what is the difference between the christian-protestant faith as expressed here, and the Catholic Faith I received in Baptism?' Father looked quite puzzled, did not answer but asked me to explain myself. 'Well Father, you are a CATHOLIC Priest. You are lecturing here to CATHOLIC Nuns and CATHOLIC parents how to pass on the CATHOLIC FAITH to our CATHOLIC children. Will you please tell me now, since you did not do that in your lecture: WHAT IS THE CATHOLIC FAITH, and what is the difference between it, and the nebulous christian faith as expressed here?' There was no answer, but the

Nuns in the audience were getting hostile with me: I SHOULD NOT HAVE ASKED THE QUESTION. It is unecumenical to highlight the difference. ...

"So, two days later after school, I went to see that Priest. He received me quite well, and only after two hours talking, during which time I reminded him, that, while he was lecturing, he was in the presence of Our Lord, Our Lady, and all the Martyrs who had died for the difference between protestant and Catholic Faith, did he tell me that he did not really know the difference, but that there had to be one. So we went to Vatican I: 'Fide Divina ET CATHOLICA ...', the Divine AND CATHOLIC FAITH, once again teaching us and taking further, what had already been taught authoritatively by TRENT.

"I include this little episode because I am becoming exceedingly hostile to the brazen way in which official CATHOLIC doctrine is being suppressed, mutilated and made unrecognisable. Vatican I, echoed by our present Holy Father Pope Paul VI, in *Mysterium Fidei* (no 24, never quoted) has clearly told us once and for all that 'the same signification of Sacred Dogmas is to be forever retained once our holy Mother the Church has defined it, and under no pretext of deeper penetration may that meaning be weakened'. (Const. Dogmat. DE FIDE **CATHOLICA**).

"Now TRENT and VATICAN I have clearly established that Faith, in order to be Divine, Life-giving and Redemptive in its own right, is the FIDES CATHOLICA. All other faith, including any sort of nebulous christian faith, shall not be redemptive in its own right, but only insofar as it somehow shares in Catholic Faith. Under no pretence of deeper penetration may CATHOLIC Faith be substituted for CHRISTIAN faith. Yet that is done everywhere, causing the greatest confusion."

So far my notes to Rome. This episode showed that the Beyerhaus effect was immediate as soon as the question of orthodoxy was put in the context of the gathering, showing that the climate that was being 'woven' was NOT orthodox. It gave the Priest and the Nuns an opportunity to reveal what they were already thinking privately and to go over it later on in calmer moments. It gave me the opportunity 'to go after that Priest'. He soon afterwards gave up his association with the 'christian formation lectures' to find more rewarding work to do. His notes show that any united world religion and any intercommunion could be built on them. It is pure equivocation to talk about the Eucharist in catholic and protestant sense, and then to teach that 'the Eucharist' is the centre of all christian life ... as if protestants have the Eucharist.

(B) The First Australian Conference of Catholic Laity

This Sydney-based Conference, held from April 23-26, 1976, was meant to be the 'Bangkok Conference' for Australian Catholicism: a conference, where 'spiritual marxism' would become acceptable to catholics in Australia. After having watched for more than seven years the unremitting dilution of things catholic in Australia, I was convinced that only marxist catholics need a conference like that to firm their grip on the Sacred in order that they can be recognised as the 'new breed Fuhrers' to the united world religion of the one-world church. The organisers did not endear themselves to the true Catholic Church in Australia with their pre-conference 'Banner': 'The Catholic Church in Australia': a book so thoroughly reprehensible that the Melbourne Conference Executive returned the 400 copies forthwith back to Sydney. With that booklet the planners showed their hand, and from then on things fell into place and resistance against them became possible. After all, they did not ask us to centre our thoughts and discussions around the teachings of the Church, but to use THEIR strange syncretism as the basis for our regional and national conferences ... With this pamphlet the tone of the conference AS REQUIRED BY THE ORGANISERS, was set. In line with this, the first plenary session, requested by the large Melbourne delegation

Chapter Two: The Detection and Destruction of 'SM' 67

so that conference could decide **its own** format and schedule, was characterised by at least 5 glaring omissions, departing from any proper conference procedures.

i. The agenda was deliberately vague and kept till the very last so that prior study and debate on it became impossible.
ii. There were no orderly, proper safeguards for debate right from the start. Everybody, including observers, could jump up at any time and address the gathering at will and at length.
iii. Like for Bangkok, the Sydney planners had aimed for a fractionalised conference, mainly consisting of endless group discussions. There was no advanced warning that these groups would be selected by a most unusual method open to fraud. Surprise was essential so that any objection that could be raised would have no time to take effect 'because of a tight schedule to be kept'.

iv. There was deliberate and complete silence on how information was going to be handled, whose property it was and how it was going to be submitted to the press. In a fragmented conference as was planned for in Sydney, strong, conference guidelines in this matter are essential. They were completely absent.

v. Finally, that first night, there was absolutely no warning from the chair (there hardly was a 'chair'): (a) about the freedom of the conference to decide its own format. This freedom was strongly RESENTED by the chairman. (b) About the consequences of FRAGMENTATION. (c) About the results of the 'free for all' atmosphere and 'let the Spirit guide us'. In other words there was no outline by the chair of BALANCE, PERSPECTIVE, FRAMEWORK, CHOICES and CONSEQUENCES. In other words there was not even an elementary HONESTY. Just a tenacious driving towards fragmentation, towards a preconceived plan,

> against any opposition, now matter how legitimate. And then they say it took two years to plan this conference ...

We can imagine what happened when, into this 'fabric', Papal teaching, or devotion to Our Lady were introduced. The 'Beyerhaus effect' became immediately observable. The workshop on 'christian family life' was deadlocked for hours over the Papal Encyclical *Humanae Vitae*: 7 accepting the teaching of the Church as the basis for this workshop, 7 dissenting from Papal teaching and rejecting it as a basis for the workshop discussions. Had the encyclical not been introduced, and the discussions conducted along the lines set out by the pre-conference pamphlet, ON THE ADVICE OF THE SAME PAMPHLET, modernism and dissent would have been the result, and no Beyerhaus effect would have been the result.

The effect the inclusion of Devotion to Our Lady and the daily Rosary in the Liturgy paper had on the marxist catholics present at Sydney I have already revealed in the pages of the Brisbane 'Catholic Leader'. It is Pope Paul's expressed wish that the devotion to Our Lady is directly related to the Holy Eucharist, where Her Son and Her God is bodily present, just as much the result of Her Faith and Her Fiat as His presence amongst His people 2000 years ago. She is eminently capable of perfecting the laity's share in the Priesthood of Christ: the centre of the liturgy in the Catholic Church. All this is just as much lost on people who want to 'BUILD THE EARTH' (Teilhard), as 'building the earth' is lost on Our Lady. The 'Beyerhaus Effect' was immediate.

From the taped recordings of the proceedings of this discussion, it is made abundantly clear that the only objection to this paper was the inclusion of the recommendations of the devotion to Our Lady. If it was disgraceful that 32 Catholics at a conference of the CATHOLIC laity saw fit to vote against the Devotion to Our Lady: even more abject was the fact that these protesters stipulated that their protest vote be recorded in the official records of the conference. This means that these dissenters have no longer only to deal with orthodox catholics: they have challenged the Blessed Virgin Mary, and they now have to deal directly with the Mother of God,

Chapter Two: The Detection and Destruction of 'SM'

who narrowly retained Her rightful place at the first national conference of catholic laity in 1976.

What was at stake here in this Sydney Conference? Whoever wrote, inspired and recommended the pre-conference booklet, showed that the feeding ground of radicals is not the Catholic Church (never mind the pious invocations of the Holy Spirit every five minutes), not Our Lady, not the Blessed Sacrament, or the Rosary, or the Communion of Saints or 'prayer and penance' Fatima style: they are fed from a totally different background which is menacingly real and uncomfortably close.

The real power-base of radicals within (the visible confines of) the Catholic Church are dissenting catholics, and at stake in Sydney was THE STATUS OF DISSENTING CATHOLICS. These catholics must at all cost be kept within those visible confines of the Church. It is the vowed intention of radical catholics that dissenters from Papal teaching MUST BE GIVEN EQUAL STATUS WITH BELIEVERS. A lot more will be heard about this in the future.

It is now become a distinct possibility – through the foreshadowed formation of a National Pastoral Council – that a Bishop will find himself with one orthodox priest and two marxist priests and with one orthodox layman and two marxist ones IN THE ONE WORKSHOP in mortal combat about this very point: the status of dissenters from *Humanae Vitae* within the Catholic Church. The National Pastoral Council was the only thing the radical element wanted desperately to emerge from the Sydney conference. On National Pastoral Councils Bishops are a minority, and through such councils radicals can consolidate their grip on the Sacred. The 'Beyerhaus Effect' at the Sydney Laity Conference showed that this 'grip' is most undesirable since it does not come from God.

(C) The Christian Family Groups in the Perth Archdiocese

What follows here is of the utmost importance since it has a direct link with the previously discussed conference of catholic laity in Sydney. Since it is a public matter it will be discussed here to prove the point made earlier.

1. JIM MIOLIN was a delegate from the Perth Archdiocese to the Sydney National Conference of Catholic Laity of Australia.
2. In a certain parish bulletin of Perth it was officially announced that Jim Miolin would speak one evening in the parish hall on the formation of christian family groups.
3. The public meeting was held. During that meeting Jim Miolin was asked two questions:

    a. Will these groups consist of catholics only?
    b. Are the groups formed so that catholics can help each other to live up to the teaching of the Church, especially the teaching of *Humanae Vitae* regarding contraception?

4. The 'BEYERHAUS EFFECT' was immediate. Showing the type of 'spirituality' that was being woven. In the presence of the Parish Priest, Jim Miolin rejected Papal teaching as the basis for his groups

for the reason that it was too controversial ... Members of the audience turned on the questioner, who was told in no uncertain terms where he could go with his 'difficulties'. 'If he looked at it more closely' Jim Miolin told him, 'he would find that *Humanae Vitae* was not even in the mind of Christ ...'

5. At the same time Jim disclosed that he had been officially appointed to carry out his 'apostolate' of the formation of 'christian family groups' over the whole Archdiocese of Perth, and that the Archbishop was expected to contribute $1500 towards it.

It is developments like these which force other catholics to disclose what is going on. Jim Miolin revealed himself at that meeting as a dissenter from Papal teaching. That is, strictly speaking, his own business. He did not become one overnight at Sydney: it is reasonable to assume that he went to Sydney as a dissenter, and that he hoped that his dissent would be consolidated by the Conference. This did not turn out as he expected. On the contrary: Jim Miolin's own workshop on 'CHRISTIAN FAMILY LIFE' opened its paper on 'SEXUALITY AND MARRIAGE' with these words:

> This Conference accepts the teachings of Vatican II, *Humanae Vitae*, and the *Declaration on Sexual Ethics* in relation to marriage, the family and the preservation of human life, and views with concern the fact that some members of the Church find difficulty in accepting the official teachings of the Church on contraception.

As a catholic and as a delegate, Jim was bound to uphold and implement this teaching and this resolution. That he does NOT, and declared his unwillingness openly when questioned, makes his dissent a public matter. Everyone in the Archdiocese of Perth knows he was a Conference Delegate, and that he was officially appointed to his 'apostolate'. The implementation of his PRIVATE dissent as PUBLIC POLICY can now be taken by everyone else AS THE OFFICIAL POLICY OF THE SYDNEY CON-

FERENCE. That is totally unacceptable. That is rejected by Jim as too controversial, as not being in the Mind of Christ. What on earth does he think will be in the Mind of Christ? His own 'spiritual marxism'? But that is only in the mind of the 'cosmic-christ': that non-existing figment of Teilhard's evolutionary imagination.

Conclusion

It is not easy to write about subversion. Neither is it easy to remain silent when all around us good and sincere catholics are being made to believe that dissent and 'spiritual marxism' are the accepted teachings of Vatican II and portray to us 'what is in the mind of Christ', when all that can be said about it is that it is heresy linked with the teilhardian subversion for the establishment of the one-world 'church of darkness'.

We are reminded of the words of St. Paul: WHERE ANOTHER Jesus is proclaimed by another gospel, another spirit is also present there (2 Cor. 11:4). With this passage St. Paul goes to the heart of the modern problem: the marxists everywhere are trying to paralyse any opposition against them by proclaiming the 'gospel' that the Spirit is working everywhere in the world, including in marxist revolutions and attempts to wipe out injustice. According to St. Paul, this is 'another gospel' and so 'another spirit' is present.

It is true that the Holy Spirit is working in marxists FOR THEIR CONVERSION, but NOT through their works ... 'What the Spirit brings is very different', says St. Paul in his letter to the Galatians, and in innumerable other places in his writings, forestalling any claim bad people may lay on the Holy Spirit.

St. John goes even further, in his second letter, when he writes:

"IF ANYONE COMES TO YOU BRINGING YOU 'ANOTHER GOSPEL', YOU MUST NOT RECEIVE HIM IN YOUR HOUSE, OR EVEN GIVE HIM A GREETING. TO GREET HIM WOULD MAKE YOU A PARTNER IN HIS WICKED WORK."

And the Apostle of Love was known to have shown BY EXAMPLE that he practised what he preached. There is not a shadow of a doubt that the Church has always reserved Her most severe penalties for the ones 'who bring another gospel'.

We Catholics must use authentic Church teaching, or Our Lady, or the teaching of Pope Paul to

Conclusion

probe any given situation, and if a hostile reaction is shown, or ridicule, or rejection, we must take the matter further and show our concern for our fellow men: the other victims present and the misguided deceivers as well. It means we must study up on our religion and know our Faith, and the teachings of the Church, and of Pope Paul, in order to know the difference. But that is all to the good and will make us better apostles.

The true ecumenism, announced by the Second Vatican Council, built on Truth, fruit of the Holy Spirit, and found very close to Our Lady, Mother of the Church, is a very delicate plant indeed, and is the exact opposite of the noisy, false replica, which is weaving its web right around the world, requesting of catholics to just stand back and watch the marxists and teilhardians and modernists take over and unite the whole world in a United World Religion ON THE SUPPRESSION OF TRUTH, with the exclusion of Our Lady, but 'assuredly coming from the Holy Spirit ...'

> "Do not harness yourselves in an uneven team with unbelievers. Virtue is no compan-

ion for crime. Light and darkness have nothing in common. Christ is not the ally of Beliar, nor has a believer anything to share with an unbeliever. The temple of God has no common ground with idols. And that is what we are, the temple of the living God: we have God's word for it.

"Then come away from them, and keep aloof, says the Spirit. Touch nothing that is unclean and I will welcome you and be your Father, and you shall be My sons and daughters, says the Almighty Lord'." (2 Cor. 6:14-17)

www.ingramcontent.com/pod-product-compliance
Lightning Source LLC
Chambersburg PA
CBHW060347050426
42449CB00011B/2858